Internal Medicine

poems by

To Lucille + Isaac,
The best in-laws in the
world! Thanks for everything—
especially "Aaron"!
With love, admiration
+ gratitude,

Susan
Shapiro

Susan Shapiro

IM Press

First Printing 1997

Manufactured in the United States of America

IM Press
P.O. Box 5346
Takoma Park, Maryland 20913-5346

Autographed copies of this book can be ordered through
IM Press at the above address. Send a $10.00 check
(includes postage and handling) for each copy **ordered**.

Library of Congress Catalog Card Number: 97-70992

ISBN 0-9654651-1-X

Cover design and artwork by Rina Drucker Root
Back cover photo by Daniel Root
All rights reserved by artists.

Thanks to Gina Kehayoff at Gina Kehayoff Verlag KG for use of the
cover photo which first appeared on Serge Bramly's "Anonym."

Acknowledgements:
Some of these poems first appeared in *Poetry East*, *The Bridge*,
Present Tense, *Jewish Frontier*, *Lilith*, *Cover*, *Downtown*, *The
Aquarian* and *Cosmoploitan*.

To My Mother & Father

CONTENTS

Father's Skeleton

Slavic Eye

Unborn Souls Choose Their Mothers

CONTENTS

My Pink Closet

Hot Woman in the Tropics

Dream House

FATHER'S SKELETON

MEDICAL SCHOOL

for my brother Brian

I saw him pass you pieces:
"Humerous, radius, carpus, ulna"
I traced along my arm as he
handed you the brittle yellow puzzle:
"Remember the tibia, femur and fibula"
like a nursery rhyme I missed
while you danced his skeleton
to your room and locked the door
that night father gave you his bones.

TRANSPARENCY

Pretending chest pains
so you'd hear me with your
stethoscope, hold me up to
your lit screen and see inside

the cloudy skeleton with only
heart shadow, nothing visibly
torn or broken, vacant
sockets for eyes

Now I too study internal
medicine: connecting
caverns of bones, shared
blood, blindness as metaphor

UNCLE SID AT THE SUKKOTH PARTY

So I lost my Social Security check the Cossacks
are at it again I'm telling you I won Jersey Lotto
last year seven and a half million but the lady
at the grocery lost my dollar and number she stole it
to tell God's truth and changed her name. If I die
tomorrow and the state sends me papers address them
to my grave why don't you I hate holidays and when she
comes to sit shiva tell her even if she forgot the number
when I was a kid in Poland you didn't do that to friend.

GRANDPA'S ACCOUNT

Shirley died last winter. See, I wrote
December 3 on this paper. Mama died in June
of 1916. Six months ago I sold my condo but
those ten percent real estate Chozzers never
paid. Promises are no good, I keep a list.
My wife Yetta went September '72. My sister
died at birth in 1910, I had a twin you know.
Twenty grand they owe me for the condo, said
it's in the mail. Gonif, so where's my check?
My daughter Shirley's gone, they took everything.
I should fly back to Lauderdale and punch them
in the face. I used to write poems too in Jewish,
three dollars each they gave me to print them
in the newspaper so you'd better watch out
or they'll steal all that's left. Remember
Papa died in '27, then they took Shirley.

SHAPIRO'S WINDOW SHADES

for my father

On a rainy afternoon inside
your father's storefront on Delancey,
you stood against coarse fabric
and told him you were leaving,
swore you'd wasted enough years
lugging blinds up broken steps.
He wound a linen sheet around its roller.

Down flights of subway stairs
in the sweater that smells of your cigars
I return by heart to the empty lot
where his tenement held
the dusty shades of missing
fathers, as if we could recover
the "Shapiro & Son" sign
he made but never showed you.

INTERNIST

My father gave his father blood
then held the silver disk
to his heart and listened closely.
"You're no good. You're killing me."

My father played his father a rare
recording of "Meine Yiddishe Mama."
Grandpa sang until the end, turned
and said, "The other version was better."

My father told Rabbi Stern
his father never forgave him
for studying medicine, leaving
"Shapiro's Windowshades" on Delancey.

My father found his two favorite
medical school professors buried
at the same cemetery. "Even your father's
mentors were mean," my mother told me.

"No man in his life told your father
I'm proud of you." At the grave
he took my mother's hand and said
"All my fathers are dead now."

GAMES MY FATHER TAUGHT ME

1

While you sleep I turn on lights in your den.
If I could reach the highest shelf, past
World War II, Cancer, Jewish History,
I would touch the blue anthology
of poetry, you tested me.

2

Thirty years later I still recite
your rule: "If you drop a book
kiss it, sacred like the Torah."

3

Playing "Disease" at dinner, you served up
symptoms: "Forty-year-old vomiting blood."
My pre-Med brothers offered "Schistosomiasis?"
"Stomach ulcer?" I said haikus, sonnets
with uneven rhymes. You said "Go sell
your poems on the sidewalk."

4

But that afternoon you pounded your fist,
sang the line "I spit into the Face
of Time..." I yelled back
"That has transfigured me!"
You said "I made up the memory."

5

Sneaking away from cousin Shelley's wedding
for a cigarette outside the synagogue,
drunk on White Russians you whisper
"You're doing what I was afraid to."

SLAVIC EYE

THE GHOST OF AUNT ROSE

Uncle Mayshe was walking down the aisle,
giving his youngest Shelley away
when I saw Rose
holding onto his other arm
as if nothing had happened.
She just swept past
in her low-cut lilac gown
with hair dark as her daughter's.
Under branches vows were taken,
the wedding glass shattered.
My mother took my hand and whispered
"I would come back too."

IF CELIA WROTE NATIE A LETTER

It makes no sense but I can't stop eating brisket
burned the way you like with stuffing and potatoes.
Dr. Stern says two hundred pounds ain't good at my age.
I told him my husband's dead and the Clinton Clubhouse
is boarded up where we used to go dancing.
You yelled "Ceil's got the best legs on Delancey"
and I did and they all said so.

I guess it's better without you losing money
all the time, coughing like an ox in your sleep.
One night I screamed "Shut up already" and Helene says
"Ma, you're dreaming." She's still got a big mouth.
Took me to Atlantic City for my birthday.
I played slots like you taught me but got apples and limes.
Rorie's six now. When I talk to you he says I'm crazy.
I say you don't spend forty-six years listening to someone
and then just stop hearing.

BY HEART
for Aunt Ettie

Kicking off light blue heels
you led the Hora
at cousin Shelley's wedding.
"You're sad again, Shoshana."
You danced me from my corner
into circle after circle.

The night I ran away
you found me in the basement.
We said the shadow poem
french-inhaling your
Pall Mall menthols
and never told.

When your husband died you said
"The Goodman women are strong."
Downstairs I stole a cigarette
sang "I had a little shadow"
like a prayer, trying on
your pretty Russian veil.

AUNT REBA'S HOUSE IN FAIR LAWN

I didn't want to be here last year, the year before &
don't want to be here now, Uncle Solly with his camera
shooting Aunt Ettie & smoked herring in the kitchen,
Cousin Louie from Belmar asks when I'm getting married,
Aunt Celia with an extra plate for her dead husband Natie,
"May he rest in peace the bum." Where's cousin Shelley,
"just too busy with her own life I suppose" to come.
I go to the wall of Goodman photos & find myself inside the
frame at someone's marriage, burial or bar mitzvah. Again
there's too much food & flashcubes keep catching me like a
guilty bystander at the scene of a crime. "She's looking at
the pictures again," Aunt Reba says, calling me to kitchen.
I walk out of the photograph, join my family at the table.

THE ARTIST

for Bette

Your delicate hands recast your history:
naked figure in onyx you christened
"Girl in Sorrow," beside the bronze
"Aphrodite" on your window ledge
like a bodyguard. I visit the faceless
women in your windswept studio where I
watched you mold a sleek Marplex lady,
thick hands covering her head as if to
hide weeping, that day you told me how
your mother Lilly took you to Russia
when you were four to rendezvous with
her lover, leaving you at the hotel in
that cold country, alone, without language.

HILDA & DIANE'S SING-A-LONG

Two ninety-year-old sisters from Essex Street
teach music every Thursday at three-thirty.
Hilda hands out the lyrics she's typed.
Diane plays the white piano, leading
thirty old crooners in new renditions
of "Blue Tango" and "How High the Moon."
After class Diane speaks of Julliard, Russia,
her dead husbands, braiding my long hair
while Hilda nods, gathering back her songs.

HOW MT PARENTS MET

HERS

At the Henry Street party I wore my hot
pink sweater. He was standing with Lefty
smoking cigarettes in the corner,
said he went to City College
but Selma knew better.
I told him I didn't like liars,
dated older men not troublemakers.
He was handsome like a gangster.

HIS

I was playing ball at the Alliance,
she was rooting for the wrong team
and talking to Steinberg. I saw
her hair was red, same as her nails.
Lefty said she lived on the corner of Clinton,
went to Seward Park High with Selma.
She wore a dress with green buttons.
I walked her home for hours.

GRANDMOTHER SOPHIE

The silence tells me it's Sabbath
on Delancey. I'm peering
through tenement windows
for a woman with high cheekbones
who undoes the thick bun that binds
her dark hair.

I never met Sophie,
the dead woman whose face I stole
from the photograph
that scared me as a child.
My mother whispered
"The Goodman women are witches."

I hold back my hair dark as blackbread.
"Grandmother, I'm hexed again."
Lightning on the Lower East Side
the Goodman blood rises to my cheeks
and Sophie on the fire escape
winks a Slavic eye.

UNBORN SOULS CHOOSE
THEIR MOTHERS

TO MY MOTHER

Your kitchen, your passion
for matzah brei, your family
sharing the bread of affliction.
I ate in my room, inside
the pink wallpaper you'd chosen.
In my dreams I set fire to your
flowered apron and thick hair.

Next to you that Passover seder
I cursed our profiles
in the cut glass mirror.
Refusing to help you serve
I left your table,
could not return
when you called to me.

Now I walk back in to the kitchen
to find you lighting
the Yahrzeit candle for your mother.
All night we eat and play scrabble,
words and emotions twisted
like the challah bread
we break and break between us.

MOVING TO NEW YORK

You didn't warn me this flight could kill me.
I left you hours early to avoid the storm.
Now the woman beside me makes the sign
Of the Cross. Red flashes and lightning,
I lock myself in, regret everything, remember
My fear of thunder, feigning nightmares
So you'd rush in with Yiddish songs and never leave.
"Rojinkes mit mandlen..." I tricked you to save me.
Lights back on, the stewardess asks if I'm hungry,
The sky soft again, blue, deceptively clear.

ARGUMENT WITH MY MOTHER

I spent years cutting myself out
of photographs. When I visit home
you hide the albums, afraid
I'll destroy the hideous faces
you'll show my new lovers.
While you sleep I sneak
to the basement to take back
my childhood. I touch the scissors.
You storm in, seize the evidence
and turn your perfect face
to the stairs shrieking
"You were always so pretty and happy!"

DEPARTURE

Suddenly all these women with red hair cut
like my mother's. Yet I'm lying in a hidden
bed next to the man with hundreds of hands.
My clothes are disappearing and he offers
love and passion when I hear myself summoned
to the kitchen for a tea party of red heads.
I make myself a tomato omelet one of them
grabs away. Hey! I want his hands and my
breakfast but the red women dance the Hora
around me. "Go away! You're crazy!" I wake up
hungry and call him. He says "It's a good omen."

LOST DAUGHTER

You wanted my milk,
my father's rare blood,
Grandmother Sophie's thick hair.

I wanted my empty body.

Now you're trapped,
kicking as if you
still hold me.

I refuse you again.

Your sharp bones slip inside
the night's mirror, demanding
eyes dark as mine.

TRICK

Two short white sheets with sneakers
ring the front doorbell.
I scavenge kitchen counters:
no candy, no apples.

Through the window I watch
the last October breeze
killing the flame inside
the pumpkin across the street.

Small ghosts I can't feed
wave, then fly away.

SELF-SERVING

She makes a lot of herself, sends four home
to her mother in Michigan, one to Rabbi Adler,
faxes three to Aunt Celia for the holidays
in Florida, mails a bunch to her high school
alumni newsletter, slips a couple to tip
the foreign cab driver, hands out a stack
like fliers to strangers on Fifth Avenue,
stashes a few away for future lovers
as her outline gets lighter, she's so good
but getting better at giving herself away.

UNBORN SOULS CHOOSE THEIR MOTHERS

I'm looking for Mimi, the orphan you were
on the Lower East Side, holding your
photograph, catching your sad Russian
eyes as they keep catching mine.

Faint voices lead up
the fire escape. Above the end
of Sabbath noise, two girls
sit on the stairs
whispering of Yeshiva boys
and sneaking cigarettes.

I keep missing Mimi, girl with your face
escaping down the steps of your old tenement
where we met once decades before mother
or daughter was decided.

MY PINK CLOSET

GIRLFRIENDS

for Stacey

Motown, our town, we sang
"Stop in the name of love"
our palms stop signs
your breasts bigger
car wheels crushed
the gravel behind us.

Past lawns of yellow grass
No Pest Strips sagged against
the end of August
we threw off clothes
dared each other into
the cold and dirty water.

Your family leaving again
we linked arms in darkness
backward two-steps, watch out
the tunnel of branches
Quick, one last smoke
"Before you break my heart..."

Walking barefoot
to the man-made beach
we swore, puffed Viceroys
in the sun and painted each other's
toe nails blue on the edge
of the broken picnic table.

LATE MEETING

for my brother Michael

I can tell you're not asleep.
The others born between us
never knew. Four in the morning
I sneaked downstairs, put
my ear to the door, heard
the rustling of negatives.

Slipping into your darkroom
we developed images, still
trying to master the night,
photographer and poet,
the first and last child
man with my eyes.

WANDERING JEWS

for my brother Eric

King Solomon with freckles,
you mediated a land war on the playground
then treated the whole third grade
to red and blue rocket popsicles.

Now you survey the basement, searching
drawers and cabinets for our home
movies, those silver circles
of your distant reign.

I find the film, play you again among
comrades. That afternoon the world fit,
I should have warned you: the moving van
outside, the shock of exile.

MISSING

The rest of the grade played
kickball on the blacktop
close to the classroom
while she sat in the dirt
far away from the noise.

By the woods in back
of the playground where no one
dared hurt her, she threaded
each tiny piece past
the silver needle's eye.
Black-blue-white-black-blue-red...
a spy memorizing an essential pattern.

Trying to finish her chain
she braided strands, studying
the distance, the hours, how much
allowance it would cost,
this precise art
of protection.

When the bell rang someone tripped
her bead-box tumbled and she
fell to her knees to save
what she could, knowing
she was leaving important
colors behind.

CONFESSION

I took off all my clothes at recess.
By lunch the whole first grade knew.

Twenty-five years later I admit
I was the sinner, star and the tattle-tale.

I have never been good at secrets,
unbutton my self heedlessly.

Still it was so easy, owning
that playground, for hours.

EARLY STAGES

for SC

1

A reckless virgin, I enter your bedroom
without knocking, peeling off pink
pantyhose like a snake on the carpet.
Drunk on my mother's hidden sherry
I watch myself in every mirror, eyelids
painted lilac, I turn on lights and scratch
your back with long nails I still grow because
that night you said you liked them.

2

All girls keep things: Compact mirrors,
pressed flowers. I'll collect
condom wrappers. Each time you leave
I'll retrieve them from the garbage,
stuff them in a shopping bag
in the basement. When you're gone
for good I'll sneak downstairs
and build a foil house from
the love we make so often.

3

In dreams you're killed in a freak accident,
sleeping with my friend Francesca whom
you've never met, exiled to El Salvador
where I scrawl you desperate
poems on purple paper as if we're divorcing:
dividing furniture and children. I slow dance
holding dead flowers in the mirror,
homesick in my own room.

LAST NOTE FROM GABRIELLE

Here's the deposit back and keys, Gorgeous
I've been meaning to tell you
I've been sleeping with Steve since November.
Hope you don't mind, I borrowed your
purple sweater, showed him your poetry
in bed, he wasn't surprised. He loves you.
My father's 80 today, my mother hates him.
The May phone bill's due on the 15th.
I wish I was better but don't regret living
with you, it gave me discretion.
Hard to believe it's all over. Call me
remember I'm not inconsistent.

REUNION

Back in my pink closet, ransacking
boxes at three A.M. I light a Belvedere
from a fourteen-year-old pack. Under piles
of doll clothes I'm shocked to find
old Barbie, bare, red-headed
like my mother, with pen eyeliner;
her husband Dr. Ken and their
four naked Little Kiddles,
noses chopped off. Dark
daughter Francie wears nothing
but safety pin earrings, still holding
her army surgeon boyfriend
GI-Joe, stolen from my brothers.
The six Dawn doll cheerleaders are so tiny
instead of changing their clothes
I just switched their heads.
By sunrise, dizzy from the stale
cigarettes, I comb their hair,
unbend arms and legs, refasten
little buttons on pants and coats
until they're dressed to kill.
I try to sleep but from the shelf
they glare, beady eyes hiding all
I left tangled there.

HOT WOMAN IN THE TROPICS

SUNSCREEN

We should be making love
but I'm confined to shade
in Negril reading a dim affair
from Italy. You're a bronzed fish
fluttering around the deep
as if nothing's wrong
with a hot woman in the tropics lost
in a second rate translation.

You leap off cliffs, shout
"Eels! Barracudas!" and surface with
treasures: striped shells, brain coral.
I'll join you under the water
after essays by an Asian feminist
or maybe I'll lend you a slow book
of sadness set in Ecuador
so we can share the same journey.

Roosters and reggae at dawn, I feel
you and the masks missing.
I reach for a West Indian poet
by the bed, about to render
this new language, revealing
a white girl at the edge
of the window in only your
bone ring and yesterday's burn.

ECHO

That summer in Tel Aviv we argued, slept
on separate beaches with other bodies
beside the same sea. All night
the white waves wrestled in anger.
In the last blue darkness before dawn
we put our ears to different shells,
heard the idiot noise of our denial
on the ancient sands of Zion, where
we were supposed to be free.

EXORCISM

Vacuumed up the tiny worry dolls you brought back
from Haiti, rescued the red one with severed arms.
On second thought tossed your whole voodoo set
into the garbage. Caught your green tee-shirt
from Belize inside my pink angora sweater.
Are you cold without me? Wearing nothing
but yourself and getting that wrong? I light
your long candles in my new one-bedroom.
Stories higher, a taller man on his way
over, burning all night to spite you.

BELOW ZERO

Coldest night of the year, windchill
so literal. Buried blue sweater, your
old hiking boots, orange flowered shirt
from Tahiti where I've never been.
I've been warmer, wearing less.
Frozen in the full-length mirror
I try on everything you
left from every angle. If I fall
asleep in your clothes
I won't dream of you.

WINDOWS

for GR

Blue lovers escape
through a forest of lilies
descend with angels, blaze
naked with baskets of fruit
in the riot of spring.

A dim corner: donkeys,
lost jugglers, purple clowns
circle a man with seven fingers
locked in a mirror
with a pregnant woman.

In the shadow of Chagall
your fear has seven fingers.
Still her upside down head of flowers
fills the last astonished
village with light.

NOT RELATED
for HS

"We're not dating. You don't have the right
to destroy my table," said the gray-bearded
poet with my last name after I absent-mindedly
overshot the ashtray when I twisted out
my cigarette, leaving a small burn.

Breezing through a sheaf of my rough
pages, he couldn't possibly know
all the former lovers' possessions I had
accidentally ruined, broken, unraveled,
ripped off in passion.

Today we ate fried eggs and kasha at his favorite
Brooklyn Heights diner but really I came
to touch his books, finger his jackets,
read his words like my words though
wiser, terser, bound in leather.

Not sure what to call this visiting girl
he told his friends who stopped by our booth
"This is my niece from the Village," or
"Have you met my daughter?" Last time
he called me his second cousin.

In his living room I took his torn
blue paperback collections from the shelf
called "Battle Reports." He signed it,
kissed me on the lips at the door,
said "Published before you were born."

DELIVERY

Ripping past your name, I run
fingers over leaves and fragile
petals, slicing off the ends
at an angle, trusting flowers
to lie. But your white tulips
arrive desperate, silky faces swooning
toward the window, necks swept over
the sharp edges of crystal,
tall green legs tangled together
in a mime of longing, thirsty
for even this dim light.

FROM A YOUNG WOMAN OF AMBITION

It's a shame we can't meet for coffee
recite Lowell and Rich and Roethke the way we did
when I was a Midwest refugee in love
with your city.

Two bottles of cheap wine on your dusty floor
you said I talked too much too loud too fast:
"Don't be nervous we're not having
an affair or anything."

You fixed all my broken half-rhymes
and drew stars for honesty but advised
marriage in the end, reading my confessional
poetry as pastime.

Now you're three blocks away and pretend
you don't remember while I recapture
another guarded stanza, almost
strong enough to send

and revise my resume nightly as if achievement
were redemption and redemption
the one-bedroom in this neighborhood
I still can't afford.

Ignoring sirens across the street I turn
the page of your book in bed, read again
the last lyrical sonnet
you composed me.

DREAM HOUSE

INFECTION

Late that second summer
without you, my left eye
became inflamed, my vision blurred.
I blinked the prescribed
drops into the margin, taped
the white bandage over.
In the mirror: a good pirate.
Fearing blindness I slept for days
while it poured outside, my dreams
rerunning our final date but
this time it was funny
and I said "Keep the lamps
and all the hardcovers."
You said I looked lovely.
I said "Because I'm leaving."
I woke up alone, removed
the patch and saw a serene
September morning, no hint
of storm or tears as if
everything could be repaired.

RELAPSE

It's come back, white oval
stye under my lower left lid,
reminder: nothing painful
disappears. I can still see
your eyes are bloodshot from lying
as you swear you're not leaving.
I wake hurting, warm compress
to ease the swelling. Drops
of old medicine fall slowly,
always something wrong
in the corner, small hidden eye
within the eye, mirror
of memory, prying again.

DREAM WEDDING

In Russia. July. Inside, it's hailing.
Two overdressed families divided by rope
gossip about sex and the size of checks piled
under the chuppa. I'm wearing the wrong shade
of black—a bad omen, somebody's grandmother
tells me, my hose running down my leg.
I sneak to the ladies room for a quick
cigarette. The video people catch me
wolfing down little hotdogs and Quaaludes,
the band strikes up "Stairway to Heaven."
Silver spotlight on my waltzing parents,
my brothers handing me their yarmulkes
one at a time. I crash into a greeting line
of old lovers in light blue rented leather
jackets with their red-headed wives, hundreds
of maids-in-waiting leaping for my bouquet
which explodes into a cloud of ravens
as I escape with centerpieces just barely.

TYING THE KNOT

Like twins, you two shared red hair,
a stubborn streak and a blue room split
by toy train tracks so it's no surprise
you picked Saturday nights in November
to marry a pair of pretty Shiksehs. I ate
"Monica/Brian" and "Jill/Eric" candy
and took pictures, fumbling for the right
flash in this clan of tall female strangers.
On the dance floor I spun alone in my black
velvet dress, family witch, the last
Jewess in the world, only sister.

YOUR PRESENT
for CR

It was funny when the date stuck
for six weeks last September.
I replaced the battery twice
but the number never caught up.
"Old model," said the jeweler.
"Can't make any promises."
He gave it back to me broken.
"Not worth mending," I told you.
"So my time is up?" you said.

Final test at "Time Repairs,"
tiny shop of clocks promising
antique restoration, never "Open"
when the sign says. A blonde woman
with accent touches the watch,
says "No problem. Twenty dollars.
Leave deposit." On my return
today's date is staring. You stop by
without calling, shocked it's fixed.

DOUBLE VISION

Last night he was in a body cast. I twisted
under covers in the big white bed next to Aaron,
who doesn't sleep as close but stays.

"You were yelling in your sleep again,"
Aaron whispers in the morning,
rubbing the small of my back, following

this tangled story I keep trying
to finish off eleven years later.
"He's not dead yet," Aaron says.

DREAM HOUSE

She jumped out the screenless window or maybe
the mover accidentally nudged my black Barbie
and she fell. Pointing to a speck on the ledge
five floors below, my husband Aaron said
"Your dark self committed suicide."

"Barbie out window!" yelled my friend's daughter
Hannah, afraid she would slip too, dancing
zigzag around unpacked boxes, pressing
her face against the pain. I scrawled
a note: order screens.

Tonight black Barbie came back in a big
manilla envelope Aaron handed me at the door.
I placed her on a safer shelf, pink
one piece swimsuit perfectly in place,
long raven hair still askew.